WHOSE LIFE IS IT ANYWAY?

by

BRIAN CLARK

Dramatic Publishing
Woodstock. Illinois • London. England • Melbourne, Australia

CHART OF STAGE POSITIONS

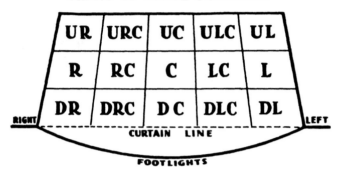

UR	URC	UC	ULC	UL
R	RC	C	LC	L
DR	DRC	D C	DLC	DL

RIGHT — CURTAIN LINE — LEFT

FOOTLIGHTS

STAGE POSITIONS

Upstage means away from the footlights, *downstage* means toward the footlights, and *right* and *left* are used with reference to the actor as he faces the audience. R means *right,* L means *left,* U means *up,* D means *down,* C means *center,* and these abbreviations are used in combination, as: U R for *up right,* R C for *right center,* D L C for *down left center,* etc. A territory designated on the stage refers to a general area, rather than to a given point.

NOTE: Before starting rehearsals, chalk off your stage or rehearsal space as indicated above in the *Chart of Stage Positions.* Then teach your actors the meanings and positions of these fundamental terms of stage movement by having them walk from one position to another until they are familiar with them. The use of these abbreviated terms in directing the play saves time, speeds up rehearsals, and reduces the amount of explanation the director has to give to his actors.

WHOSE LIFE IS IT ANYWAY?

A Full-length Play
For Nine Men and Five Women

CHARACTERS

KEN HARRISON........................ the patient
SISTER ANDERSON .... ward sister
KAY SADLER.............................. nurse
JOHN....................................... orderly
DR. JOAN SCOTT........................ doctor
DR. MICHAEL EMERSON .... consultant physician
MRS. GILLIAN BOYLE........ medical social worker
PHILIP HILL .... Ken's solicitor
DR. PAUL TRAVERS.......... consultant psychiatrist
PETER KERSHAW .... Ken's barrister
MR. JUSTICE MILLHOUSE .... judge
ANDREW EDEN................. hospital's barrister
DR. BARR .... consultant psychiatrist
NIGHT SISTER

TIME: The present.

PLACE: A hospital somewhere in England.

ACT ONE

AT RISE: *SISTER ANDERSON and NURSE KAY SADLER enter with trolley.*

SISTER. Good morning, Mr. Harrison. A new face for you today.

KEN. That's nice.

NURSE. Hello.

KEN. Hello. I'm afraid I can't offer you my hand. You'll just have to make do with my backside like all the other nurses. *(They lower the bed.)* Going down—Obstetrics, Gynecology, Lingerie, Rubber wear. *(They roll KEN over and start to massage his back and heels with spirit and talc.)* It's funny, you know. I used to dream of situations like this.

SISTER. Being injured?

KEN. No! Lying on a bed being massaged by two beautiful women.

SISTER *(mock serious)*. If you go on like this, Mr. Harrison, I shan't be able to send my young nurses in here.

KEN. They're perfectly safe with me, Sister. *(The phone rings outside.)*

SISTER. Can you manage for a moment, Nurse?

NURSE. Oh yes, Sister.

SISTER. Wipe your hands and put the pillows behind Mr. Harrison; we don't want to have him on the floor.

5

KEN. Have me on the floor, Sister, please. Have me on the floor. *(SISTER goes out.)* What's your name?

NURSE. Kay.

KEN. That's nice, but don't let Sister hear you say that.

NURSE. What?

KEN. What's your second name?

NURSE. Sadler.

KEN. Then you must answer "Nurse Sadler" with a smile that is full of warmth, but with no hint of sex.

NURSE. I'm sorry.

KEN. I'm not. I'm glad you're called Kay. I shall call you Kay when we're alone, just you and me, having my backside caressed ...

NURSE. I'm rubbing your heels.

KEN. Well, don't spoil it. After all, it doesn't matter. I can't feel anything wherever you are. Is this your first ward?

NURSE. Yes. I'm still at P.T.S.

KEN. What's that? Primary Training School?

NURSE. Yes. I finish next week.

KEN. And you can't wait to get here full time.

NURSE. I'll be glad to finish the school.

KEN. All students are the same.

NURSE. Were you a teacher?

KEN. Tut tut; second lesson. You mustn't use the past tense.

NURSE. What do you mean?

KEN. You said, "Were you a teacher?" You should have said, "Are you a teacher?" I mean, you are now part of the optimism industry. Everyone who deals with me acts as though, for the first time in the history of medical

science, a ruptured spinal column will heal itself—it's
just a bit of a bore waiting for it to happen.

NURSE. I'm sorry.

KEN. Don't be. Kay, you're a breath of fresh air.

(SISTER comes back.)

SISTER. Finished, Nurse?

KEN. What do you mean? Have I finished Nurse. I haven't
started her yet!

NURSE. Yes, Sister. *(They roll him back and remake the
bed.)*

KEN. I must congratulate you, Sister, on your new recruit.
A credit to the monstrous regiment.

SISTER. I'm glad you got on.

KEN. Well, I didn't get quite that far. Not that I didn't try,
Sister. But all I could get out of her was that her name
was...Nurse Sadler...and that she's looking forward to
coming here.

SISTER. If she still feels like that after being five minutes
with you, we'll make a nurse of her yet.

KEN. I don't know quite how to take that, Sister—lying
down, I suppose.

SISTER. Night Sister said you slept well.

KEN. Ah-thew! I fooled her...After her last round, a mate
of mine came in and smuggled me out...We went mid-
night skateboarding.

SISTER. Oh, yes...I hope it was fun...

KEN. It was all right...the only problem was that I was the
skateboard.

SISTER. There, that's better. Comfortable?

KEN. Sister, it's so beautifully made, I can't feel a thing.

SISTER. Cheerio, Mr. Harrison. *(They leave.)*

NURSE. Won't he ever get better, Sister?

SISTER. No.

NURSE. What will happen to him?

SISTER. When we have him fully stabilized, he'll be transferred to a long-stay hospital.

NURSE. For the rest of his life?

SISTER. Yes.

(JOHN, an orderly, comes along the corridor carrying shaving tackle on a tray.)

JOHN. Morning, Sister.

SISTER. Morning, John. Are you going to Mr. Harrison?

JOHN. That's right.

SISTER. He's all ready.

JOHN. Right. *(JOHN goes into the sluice room to collect an electric razor.)*

NURSE. How long has he been here?

SISTER. Four months.

NURSE. How much longer will he be here?

SISTER. Not much longer now, I should think. Take the trolley into the ward, Nurse. I should start on Mr. Phillips.

(SISTER goes into her office. JOHN goes into KEN's room. He plugs in the razor and shaves KEN.)

JOHN. Good morning, Mr. Harrison...

KEN. Come to trim the lawn?

JOHN. That's right.

KEN. Good ... Must make sure that all the beds and borders are neat and tidy.

JOHN. That's my job.

KEN. Well, my gardening friend, isn't it about time you got some fertilizer to sprinkle on me and get some movement going in this plant?

JOHN. Ah, now there you have me. You see, I'm only a laborer in this here vineyard. Fertilizers and pruning and bedding out is up to the head gardener.

KEN. Still, you must be in charge of the compost heap. That's where I should be.

(SISTER puts her head around the door.)

SISTER. John.

JOHN. Yes?

SISTER. Don't be long, will you? Dr. Scott will probably be early today; there's a consultant's round this morning.

JOHN. Right, Sister. *(SISTER goes back to her office.)*

KEN. The visitation of the Gods.

JOHN. Eh?

KEN. The Gods are walking on earth again.

JOHN. Oh, yes—they think they're a bit of all right.

KEN. What happened to the other chap—Terence he was called ... I think?

JOHN. They come and they go ... I think he left to get married up north somewhere.

KEN. Terence, getting married? Who to? A lorry driver?

JOHN. Catty!

KEN. No. Bloody jealous. From where I'm lying, if you can make it at all—even with your right hand—it would be heaven ... I'm sorry ... feeling sorry for myself this morning...can't even say I got out of the wrong side of the bed. Are you down to the bone yet?...Anyway, how long will you be staying?

JOHN. Just till we go professional, man.

KEN. Doing what?

JOHN. Music. We got a steel band—with some comedy numbers and we're getting around a bit...We're auditioning for Opportunity Knocks in four months.

KEN. That's great...Really great...I like steel bands... There's something fascinating about using oil drums—making something out of scrap...Why not try knocking a tune out of me?

JOHN. Why not, man!

(He puts down his razor and, striking KEN very lightly up and down his body like a xylophone, sings a typical steel band tune, moving rhythmically to the music. KEN is delighted. DR. SCOTT comes in. JOHN stops.)

DR. SCOTT. Don't stop...

JOHN. It's all right...I've nearly finished. *(He makes one more pass with the razor.)*

KEN. I was just making myself beautiful for you, Doctor.

JOHN. There...Finished. *(He goes to the door.)*

KEN. Work out some new tunes...Hey, if Dr. Scott could drill some holes in my head, you could blow in my ear and play me like an ocarina.

JOHN. I'll see you later. *(He grins and goes out.)*

DR. SCOTT. You're bright and chirpy this morning.

KEN *(ironically)*. It's marvelous, you know. The courage of the human spirit.

DR. SCOTT *(dryly)*. Nice to hear the human spirit's okay. How're the lungs? *(She takes her stethoscope from her pocket. She puts the stethoscope to KEN's chest.)*

KEN *(sings)*. Boom boom.

DR. SCOTT. Be quiet. You'll deafen me.

KEN. Sorry. *(She continues to listen.)* And what does it say?

DR. SCOTT *(gives up)*. What does what say?

KEN. My heart, of course. What secrets does it tell?

DR. SCOTT. It was just telling me that it's better off than it was six months ago.

KEN. It's a brave heart. It keeps its secrets.

DR. SCOTT. And what are they?

KEN. Did you hear it going boom boom, like that? Two beats.

DR. SCOTT. Of course.

KEN. Well, I'll tell you. That's because it's broken, broken in two. But each part carries on bravely yearning for a woman in a white coat.

DR. SCOTT. And I thought it was the first and second heart sounds.

KEN. Ah! Is there a consultant's round this morning?

DR. SCOTT. That's right.

KEN. I suppose he will sweep in here like Zeus from Olympus, with his attendant nymphs and swains.

DR. SCOTT. I don't think that's fair.

KEN. Why not?

DR. SCOTT. He cares; he cares a lot.

KEN. But what about?

DR. SCOTT. His patients.

KEN. I suppose so.

DR. SCOTT. He does. When you first came in he worked his guts out to keep you going; he cares.

KEN. I was a bit flip, wasn't I...

DR. SCOTT. It's understandable.

KEN. But soon we shall have to ask the question why.

DR. SCOTT. Why?

KEN. Why bother. You remember the mountain labored and brought forth not a man but a mouse. It was a big joke. On the mouse. If you're as insignificant as that, who needs a mountain for a mummy?

DR. SCOTT. I'll see you later... with Dr. Emerson.

KEN. And Cupbearers Limited.

DR. SCOTT. Oh, no...I assure you...We're not at all limited.

(She goes out. She opens the door of SISTER's room. The SISTER is writing at the desk.)

DR. SCOTT. Sister, It's Mr. Harrison. He seems a little agitated this morning.

SISTER. Yes, he's beginning to realize what he's up against.

DR. SCOTT. I'm changing the prescription and putting him on a small dose of Valium. I'll have a word with Dr. Emerson. Thank you, Sister.

(She closes the door and looks up the corridor towards KEN's room. NURSE SADLER is just going in with a feeding cup.)

KEN. An acolyte, bearing a cup.

NURSE. I beg your pardon?

KEN. Nothing. I was joking. It's nothing.

NURSE. It's coffee.

KEN. You're joking now.

NURSE. I'm not.

KEN. What you have there is a coffee-flavored milk drink.

NURSE. Don't you like it?

KEN. It's all right, but I would like some real coffee, hot and black and bitter so that I could chew it.

NURSE. I'll ask Sister.

KEN. I shouldn't.

NURSE. Why not?

KEN. Because in an hour's time, you'll be bringing round a little white pill that is designed to insert rose-colored filters behind my eyes. It will calm me and soothe me and make me forget for a while that you have a lovely body.

NURSE. Mr. Harrison ... I'm ...

KEN (*genuinely concerned*). I'm sorry. Really, I *am* sorry. I don't want to take it out on you—it's not your fault. You're only the vestal virgin ... Sorry I said virgin.

NURSE. You'd better drink your coffee before it gets cold. (*She feeds him a little, sip by sip.*)

KEN. I was right; it's milky ... What made you become a nurse?

NURSE. I'm not a nurse yet.

KEN. Oh, yes, you are. (*NURSE SADLER smiles.*) Nurse Sadler.

NURSE. You must have thought me a real twit.

KEN. Of course not!

NURSE. The Sister-Tutor told us we could say it.

KEN. Well then ...

NURSE. But I was so sure I wouldn't.

KEN. You haven't told me what made you become a nurse.

NURSE. I've always wanted to. What made you become a sculptor?

KEN. Hey there! You're learning too fast!

NURSE. What do you mean?

KEN. When you get a personal question, just ignore it—change the subject or better still, ask another question back. *(NURSE SADLER smiles.)* Did Sister-Tutor tell you that, too?

NURSE. Something like it.

KEN. It's called being professional, isn't it?

NURSE. I suppose so.

KEN. I don't want any more of that, it's horrid. Patients are requested not to ask for credit for their intelligence, as refusal often offends.

NURSE. You sound angry. I hope I...

KEN. Not with you, Kay. Not at all. With myself, I expect. Don't say it. That's futile, isn't it?

NURSE. Yes.

(SISTER opens the door.)

SISTER. Have you finished, Nurse? Dr. Emerson is here.

NURSE. Yes, Sister. I'm just coming.

SISTER. Straighten that sheet. *(She goes, leaving the door open.)*

KEN. Hospitals are weird places. Broken necks are acceptable, but a wrinkled sheet! ...

(NURSE SADLER smoothes the bed. She goes out as DR. EMERSON comes in with SISTER and DR. SCOTT.)

DR. EMERSON. Morning.

KEN. Good morning.

DR. EMERSON. How are you this morning?

KEN. As you see, racing around all over the place. *(DR. EMERSON picks up the chart and notes from the bottom of the bed.)*

DR. EMERSON *(to DR. SCOTT)*. You've prescribed Valium, I see.

DR. SCOTT. Yes.

DR. EMERSON. His renal function looks much improved.

DR. SCOTT. Yes, the blood urea is back to normal and the cultures are sterile.

DR. EMERSON. Good...Good. Well, we had better go on keeping an eye on it, just in case.

DR. SCOTT. Yes, of course, sir.

DR. EMERSON. Good...Well, Mr. Harrison, we seem to be out of the wood now...

KEN. So when are you going to discharge me?

DR. EMERSON. Difficult to say.

KEN. Really? Are you ever going to discharge me?

DR. EMERSON. Well, you'll certainly be leaving *us* soon, I should think.

KEN. Discharged or transferred?

DR. EMERSON. This unit is for critical patients; when we have reached a position of stability, then you can be looked after in a much more comfortable, quiet hospital.

KEN. You mean you only grow the vegetables here—the vegetable store is somewhere else.

DR. EMERSON. I don't think I understand you.

KEN. I think you do. Spell it out for me, please. What chance have I of only being partly dependent on nursing?

DR. EMERSON. It's impossible to say with certainty what the prognosis of any case is.

KEN. I'm not asking for a guarantee on oath. I am simply asking for your professional opinion. Do you believe I will ever walk again?

DR. EMERSON. No.

KEN. Or recover the use of my arms?

DR. EMERSON. No.

KEN. Thank you.

DR. EMERSON. What for?

KEN. Your honesty.

DR. EMERSON. Yes, well... I should try not to brood on it if I were you. It's surprising how we can come to accept things. Dr. Scott has prescribed something which will help. *(To DR. SCOTT.)* You might also get Mrs. Boyle along...

DR. SCOTT. Yes, of course.

DR. EMERSON. You'll be surprised how many things you will be able to do. Good morning. *(They go into the corridor area.)* What dose was it you prescribed?

DR. SCOTT. Two milligrams T.I.D.

DR. EMERSON. That's very small. You might have to increase it to five milligrams.

DR. SCOTT. Yes, sir.

DR. EMERSON. We ought to aim to get him moved in a month at most. These beds are very precious.

DR. SCOTT. Yes.

DR. EMERSON. Well, thank you, Doctor. I must rush off. Damned committee meeting.

DR. SCOTT. I thought you hated those.

DR. EMERSON. I do, but there's a new heart monitoring unit I want... very much indeed.

DR. SCOTT. Good luck, then.

DR. EMERSON. Thank you, Joan.

(He goes. DR. SCOTT looks in at SISTER's office.)

DR. SCOTT. Did you get that Valium for Mr. Harrison, Sister?

SISTER. Yes, Doctor. I was going to give him the first at twelve o'clock.

DR. SCOTT. Give him one now, will you?

SISTER. Right.

DR. SCOTT. Thank you. *(She begins to walk away, then turns.)* On second thought ... give it to me. I'll take it. I want to talk with him.

SISTER. Here it is. *(She hands a small tray with a tablet and a feeding cup of water.)*

DR. SCOTT. Thank you.

(She walks to KEN's room and goes in.)

DR. SCOTT. I've brought something to help you.

KEN. My God, they've got some highly qualified nurses here.

DR. SCOTT. Only the best in this hospital.

KEN. You're spoiling me, you know, Doctor. If this goes on, I shall demand that my next enema is performed by no one less than the Matron.

DR. SCOTT. Well, it wouldn't be the first she'd done, or the thousandth either.

KEN. She worked up through the ranks, did she?

DR. SCOTT. They all do.

KEN. Yes, in training school they probably learn that at the bottom of every bed pan lies a potential Matron. Just now, for one or two glorious minutes, I felt like a human being again.

DR. SCOTT. Good.

KEN. And now you're going to spoil it.

DR. SCOTT. How?

KEN. By tranquilizing yourself.

DR. SCOTT. Me?

KEN. Oh, I shall get the tablet, but it's you that needs the tranquilizing; I don't.

DR. SCOTT. Dr. Emerson and I thought...

KEN. You both watched me disturbed, worried even perhaps, and you can't do anything for me—nothing that really matters. I'm paralyzed and you're impotent. This disturbs you because you're a sympathetic person and as someone dedicated to an active sympathy doing something—anything even—you find it hard to accept you're impotent. The only thing you can do is to stop me thinking about it—that is—stop me disturbing you. So I get the tablet and you get the tranquillity.

DR. SCOTT. That's a tough diagnosis.

KEN. Is it so far from the truth?

DR. SCOTT. There may be an element of truth in it, but it's not the whole story.

KEN. I don't suppose it is.

DR. SCOTT. After all, there is no point in worrying unduly—you know the facts. It's no use banging your head against a wall.

KEN. If the only feeling I have is in my head and I want to feel, I might choose to bang it against a wall.

DR. SCOTT. And if you damage your head?

KEN. You mean go bonkers?

DR. SCOTT. Yes.

KEN. Then that would be the final catastrophe but I'm not bonkers—yet. My consciousness is the only thing I have and I must claim the right to use it and, as far as possible, act on conclusions I may come to.

DR. SCOTT. Of course.

KEN. Good. Then you eat that tablet if you want tranquillity, because I'm not going to.

DR. SCOTT. It is prescribed.

KEN. Oh, come off it, Doctor. I know everyone around here acts as though those little bits of paper have just been handed down from Sinai. But the writing on those tablets isn't Hebrew...

DR. SCOTT. ... Well, you aren't due for it till twelve o'clock. We'll see...

KEN. That's what I always say. If you don't know whether to take a tranquilizer or not—sleep on it. When you tell Dr. Emerson, impress on him I don't need it...

(DR. SCOTT smiles. She leaves and goes to the SIS-TER's room.)

DR. SCOTT. Sister, I haven't given it to him...Leave it for a while.

SISTER. Did you alter the notes?

DR. SCOTT. No...Not yet. *(She picks up a pile of notes and begins writing.)*

(CROSSFADE on sluice room. NURSE SADLER is taking kidney dishes and instruments out of the sterilizer. JOHN creeps up behind her and seizes her round the

waist. NURSE SADLER jumps, utters a muffled scream and drops a dish.)

NURSE. Oh it's you ... Don't do that ...

JOHN. I couldn't help myself, honest, my Lord. There was this vision in white and blue, then I saw red in front of my eyes. It was like looking into a Union Jack. *(NURSE SADLER has turned around to face JOHN, who has his arms either side of her against the table.)*

NURSE. Let go ...

JOHN. What's a nice girl like you doing in a place like this?

NURSE. Sterilizing the instruments ... *(JOHN gasps and holds his groin.)*

JOHN. Don't say things like that! Just the thought ... *(NURSE SADLER is free and returns to her work.)*

NURSE. I don't know what you're doing in a place like this ... It's just a big joke to you.

JOHN. 'Course it is. You can't take a place like this seriously ...

NURSE. Why ever not?

JOHN. It's just the ante-room of the morgue.

NURSE. That's terrible! They don't all die

JOHN. Don't they?

NURSE. No! Old Mr. Trevellyan is going out tomorrow, for instance.

JOHN. After his third heart attack! I hope they give him a return ticket on the ambulance.

NURSE. Would you just let them die? People like Mr. Harrison?

JOHN. How much does it cost to keep him here? Hundreds of pounds a week.

NURSE. That's not the point.

JOHN. In Africa children die of measles. It would cost only a few pounds to keep them alive. There's something crazy somewhere.

NURSE. That's wrong too—but it wouldn't help just letting Mr. Harrison die.

JOHN. No ... *(He goes up to her again.)* Nurse Sadler, when your eyes flash, you send shivers up and down my spine ...

NURSE. John, stop it ... *(She is backing away.)*

JOHN. Why don't we go out tonight?

NURSE. I've got some work to do for my exam.

JOHN. Let me help ... I'm an expert on anatomy. We could go dancing, down to the Barbados Club, a few drinks and then back to my pad for an anatomy lesson.

NURSE. Let me get on ... *(JOHN holds NURSE SADLER's head and slides his hands down.)*

JOHN *(singing)*. Oh, the head bone's connected to the
                             neck bone,
        The neck bone's connected to the shoulder
                            bone,
        The shoulder bone's connected to the ...
                            breast bone ...

(NURSE SADLER escapes just in time. She backs out of the room and into SISTER, who is coming to see what's causing the noise.)

NURSE. Sorry, Sister.

SISTER. This hospital exists to cure accidents not to cause them.

NURSE. No ... Yes ... Sister.

SISTER. Are you going to be all day with that sterilizer?

NURSE. No, Sister. *(She hurries away.)*

SISTER. Haven't you any work to do, John?

JOHN. Sister, my back is bowed down with the weight of all the work resting on it.

SISTER. Then I suggest you shift some.

JOHN. Right. *(SISTER goes. JOHN shrugs and goes.)*

(CROSSFADE on DR. EMERSON's office. DR. EMERSON is on the phone.)

DR. EMERSON. Look, Jenkins, I know the capital cost is high, but it would save on nursing costs. I've got four cardiac cases in here at the moment. With that unit I could save at least on one nurse a day. They could all be monitored in the Sister's room ... Yes, I know ...

(DR. SCOTT knocks on the door. She comes in.)

DR. EMERSON. Hello? ... Yes, well, old chap, I've got to go now. Do impress on the board how much money we'd save in the long run ... Thank you. *(He puts the phone down.)*

DR. SCOTT. Still wheeling and dealing for that monitoring unit?

DR. EMERSON. Bloody administrators. In this job, a degree in accountancy would be more valuable to me than my M.D. ... Still, what can I do for you?

DR. SCOTT. It's Harrison.

DR. EMERSON. Some sort of relapse!

DR. SCOTT. On the contrary.

DR. EMERSON. Good.

DR. SCOTT. He doesn't want to take Valium.

DR. EMERSON. Doesn't want to take it? What do you mean?

DR. SCOTT. He guessed it was some sort of tranquilizer and said he preferred to keep his consciousness clear.

DR. EMERSON. That's the trouble with all this anti-drug propaganda; it's useful of course, but it does set up a negative reaction to even necessary drugs, in sensitive people.

DR. SCOTT. I'm not sure he's not right.

DR. EMERSON. Right? When you prescribed the drug, you thought he needed it.

DR. SCOTT. Yes.

DR. EMERSON. And when I saw him, I agreed with you.

DR. SCOTT. Yes.

DR. EMERSON. It's a very small dose—two milligrams T.I.D., wasn't it?

DR. SCOTT. That's right.

DR. EMERSON. The minimum that will have any effect at all. You remember I said you might have to go up to five milligrams. A psychiatric dose, you know, is ten or fifteen milligrams.

DR. SCOTT. I know, but Mr. Harrison isn't a psychiatric case, is he?

DR. EMERSON. So how did you persuade him to take it?

DR. SCOTT. I didn't.

DR. EMERSON. Now let's get this clear. This morning when you examined him, you came to a careful and responsible decision that your patient needed a certain drug.

DR. SCOTT. Yes.

DR. EMERSON. I saw the patient and I agreed with your prescription.

DR. SCOTT. Yes.

DR. EMERSON. But in spite of two qualified opinions, you accept the decisions of someone completely unqualified to make it.

DR. SCOTT. He may be unqualified, but he is the one affected.

DR. EMERSON. Ours was an objective, his a subjective decision.

DR. SCOTT. But isn't this a case where a subjective decision may be more valid? After all, you're both working on the same subject—his body. Only he knows more about how he feels.

DR. EMERSON. But he doesn't know about the drugs and their effects.

DR. SCOTT. He can feel their effects directly.

DR. EMERSON. Makes no difference. His knowledge isn't based on experience of a hundred such cases. He can't know enough to challenge our clinical decisions.

DR. SCOTT. That's what he's doing and he's protesting about the dulling of his consciousness with Valium.

DR. EMERSON. When he came in, shocked to hell, did he protest about the dextrose-saline? Or when he was gasping for breath, he didn't use some of it to protest about the aminophylline or the huge stat dose of cortisone...

DR. SCOTT. Those were inevitable and emergency decisions.

DR. EMERSON. And so is this one inevitable. Just because our patient is conscious, that does not absolve us from our complete responsibility. We have to maximize whatever powers he retains.

DR. SCOTT. And how does a depressant drug improve his consciousness?

DR. EMERSON. It will help him to use his consciousness, Joan. We must help him now to turn his mind to the real problem he has. We must help him to an acceptance of his condition. Only then will his full consciousness be any use to him at all... You say he refused to take the tablet? *(DR. SCOTT nods. DR. EMERSON picks up the phone and dials. The phone rings in SISTER's office.)*

SISTER. Sister Anderson speaking.

DR. EMERSON. Emerson here. Could you prepare a syringe with five milligrams of Valium for Mr. Harrison?

SISTER. Yes sir.

DR. EMERSON. I'll be down myself immediately to give it to him.

SISTER. Yes sir. *(She replaces the phone and prepares the syringe.)*

DR. SCOTT. Do you want me to come?

DR. EMERSON. No... It won't be necessary.

DR. SCOTT. Thank you... *(She moves to the door.)*

DR. EMERSON. Harrison is an intelligent, sensitive and articulate man.

DR. SCOTT. Yes.

DR. EMERSON. But don't undervalue yourself. Joan, your first decision was right.

(DR. SCOTT nods and leaves the room. She is unhappy. DR. EMERSON walks to SISTER's room.)

DR. EMERSON. Have you the Valium ready, Sister?

SISTER. Yes sir. *(She hands him the kidney dish. DR. EMERSON takes it. SISTER makes to follow him.)*

DR. EMERSON. It's all right, Sister. You've plenty of work, I expect.

SISTER. There's always plenty of that.

(DR. EMERSON goes into KEN's room.)

KEN. Hello, hello, they've brought up the heavy brigade. *(DR. EMERSON pulls back the bed clothes and reaches for KEN's arm.)* Dr. Emerson, I am afraid I must insist that you do not stick that needle in me.

DR. EMERSON. It is important that I do.

KEN. Who for?

DR. EMERSON. You.

KEN. I'm the best judge of that.

DR. EMERSON. I think not. You don't even know what's in this syringe.

KEN. I take it that the injection is one of a series of measures to keep me alive.

DR. EMERSON. You could say that.

KEN. Then it is not important. I've decided not to stay alive.

DR. EMERSON. But you can't decide that.

KEN. Why not?

DR. EMERSON. You're very depressed.

KEN. Does that surprise you?

DR. EMERSON. Of course not; it's perfectly natural. Your body received massive injuries; it takes time to come to any acceptance of the new situation. Now I shan't be a minute...

KEN. Don't stick that damn thing in me!

DR. EMERSON. There... It's over now.

KEN. Doctor, I didn't give you permission to stick that needle in me. Why did you do it?

DR. EMERSON. It was necessary. Now try to sleep... You will find that as you gain acceptance of the situation you will be able to find a new way of living.

KEN. Please let me make myself clear. I specifically refused permission to stick that needle in me and you didn't listen. You took no notice.

DR. EMERSON. You must rely on us, old chap. Of course you're depressed. I'll send someone along to have a chat with you. Now I really must go and get on with my rounds.

KEN. Doctor...

DR. EMERSON. I'll send someone along. *(He places the dish on the side locker, throwing the needle in a waste bin. He goes out. KEN is frustrated and then his eyes close.)*

(CROSSFADE on SISTER's office. SISTER and DR. SCOTT are sitting.)

SISTER. I'm always warning my nurses not to get involved.

DR. SCOTT. Of course... and you never do, do you?

SISTER *(smiling)*. ...Never.

DR. SCOTT. You're a liar, Sister.

SISTER. Dr. Scott!

DR. SCOTT. Come on, we all do. Dr. Emerson is as involved with Ken Harrison as if he were his father.

SISTER. But you don't feel like his mother!

DR. SCOTT. ...No comment, Sister.

(NURSE SADLER comes into SISTER's office.)

NURSE. I've finished, Sister.

SISTER. All right ... Off you go then, Nurse.

NURSE. Yes, Sister!

SISTER. Have you been running?

NURSE. No, Sister!

SISTER. Oh ... You just looked ... flushed.

NURSE. ... Oh ... Good night, Sister ... Doctor.

SISTER / DR. SCOTT. Good night.

(CROSSFADE to KEN's room. SISTER and NURSE SADLER come in with the trolley.)

SISTER. Good morning, Mr. Harrison. How are you this morning?

KEN. Marvelous.

SISTER. Night Sister said you slept well.

KEN. I did. I had a lot of help, remember.

SISTER. Your eyes are bright this morning.

KEN. I've been thinking.

SISTER. You do too much of that.

KEN. What other activity would you suggest? ... Football? I tell you what, Sister, just leave me alone with Nurse Sadler here. Let's see what the old Adam can do for me.

SISTER. I'm a Sister not a Madame.

KEN. Sister—you dark horse you! All this time you've been kidding me. I've been wondering for months how on earth a woman could become a State Registered Nurse and a Sister and still think you found babies under a gooseberry bush—and you've known all along.

SISTER. Of course I've known. When I qualified as a mid-wife I learnt that when they pick up the babies from under the gooseberry bushes they wrap them up in women to keep them warm. I know because it was our job to unwrap them again.

KEN. The miracle of modern science! Anyway, Sister, as I said, I've been thinking, if I'm going to be around for a long time, money will help.

SISTER. It always does.

KEN. Do you remember that solicitor chap representing my insurance company a few months ago? Mr. Hill, I think he said his name was. He said he'd come back when I felt better. Do you think you could get him back as soon as possible? I'd feel more settled if we could get the compensation sorted out.

SISTER. Sounds like a good idea.

KEN. You'll ring him up?

SISTER. Of course.

KEN. He left a card; it's in my drawer.

SISTER. Right. *(She goes to the locker and takes out the card.)* Mr. Philip Hill, Solicitor. Right, I'll ring him.

KEN. Thanks.

SISTER. That's enough. *(They cover him up again and straighten the bed.)* Mrs. Boyle is waiting to see you, Mr. Harrison.

KEN. Mrs. Boyle? Who's she?

SISTER. A very nice woman

KEN. Oh God, must I see her?

SISTER. Dr. Emerson asked her to come along.

KEN. Then I'd better see her. If I refuse, he'll probably dissolve her in water and inject her into me. *(SISTER has to choke back a giggle.)*

SISTER. Mr. Harrison! Come on, Nurse; this man will be the death of me.

KEN *(cheerfully)*. Doubt it, Sister. I'm not even able to be the death of myself

(SISTER goes out with NURSE SADLER. MRS. GILLIAN BOYLE enters. She is thirty-five, attractive, and very professional in her manner. She is a medical social worker.)

MRS. BOYLE. Good morning.

KEN. Morning.

MRS. BOYLE. Mr. Harrison?

KEN *(cheerfully)*. It used to be.

MRS. BOYLE. My name is Mrs. Boyle.

KEN. And you've come to cheer me up.

MRS. BOYLE. I wouldn't put it like that.

KEN. How would you put it?

MRS. BOYLE. I've come to see if I can help.

KEN. Good. You can.

MRS. BOYLE. How?

KEN. Go and convince Dr. Frankenstein that he has successfully made his monster and he can now let it go.

MRS. BOYLE. Dr. Emerson is a first-rate physician. My goodness, they have improved this room.

KEN. Have they?

MRS. BOYLE. It used to be really dismal. All dark green and cream. It's surprising what pastel colors will do, isn't it? Really cheerful.

KEN. Yes. Perhaps they should try painting me. I'd hate to be the thing that ruins the decor.

MRS. BOYLE. What on earth makes you say that? You don't ruin anything.

KEN. I'm sorry. That was a bit...whining. Well, don't let me stop you.

MRS. BOYLE. Doing what?

KEN. What you came for, I suppose. What do you do? Conjuring tricks? Funny stories? Or a belly dance? If I have any choice, I'd prefer the belly dance.

MRS. BOYLE. I'm afraid I've left my bikini at home.

KEN. Who said anything about a bikini?

MRS. BOYLE. Dr. Emerson tells me that you don't want any more treatment.

KEN. Good.

MRS. BOYLE. Why good?

KEN. I didn't think he'd heard what I said.

MRS. BOYLE. Why not?

KEN. He didn't take any notice.

MRS. BOYLE. Well as you can see, he did.

KEN. He sent you?

MRS. BOYLE. Yes.

KEN. And you are my new treatment; get in.

MRS. BOYLE. Why don't you want any more treatment?

KEN. I'd rather not go on living like this.

MRS. BOYLE. Why not?

KEN. Isn't it obvious?

MRS. BOYLE. Not to me. I've seen many patients like you.

KEN. And they all want to live?

MRS. BOYLE. Usually.

KEN. Why?

MRS. BOYLE. They find a new way of life.

KEN. How?

MRS. BOYLE. You'll be surprised how many things you will be able to do with training and a little patience.

KEN. Such as?

MRS. BOYLE. We can't be sure yet. But I should think that you will be able to operate reading machines and perhaps an adapted typewriter.

KEN. Reading and writing. What about arithmetic?

MRS. BOYLE *(smiling)*. I dare say we could fit you up with a comptometer if you really wanted one.

KEN. Mrs. Boyle, even educationalists have realized that the three r's do not make a full life.

MRS. BOYLE. What did you do before the accident?

KEN. I taught in art school. I was a sculptor.

MRS. BOYLE. I see.

KEN. Difficult, isn't it? How about an electrically operated hammer and chisel? No, well. Or a cybernetic lump of clay?

MRS. BOYLE. I wouldn't laugh if I were you. It's amazing what can be done. Our scientists are wonderful.

KEN. They are. But it's not good enough, you see, Mrs. Boyle. I really have absolutely no desire at all to be the object of scientific virtuosity. I have thought things over very carefully. I do have plenty of time for thinking and I have decided that I do not want to go on living with so much effort for so little result.

MRS. BOYLE. Yes, well, we shall have to see about that.

KEN. What is there to see?

MRS. BOYLE. We can't just stop treatment, just like that.

KEN. Why not?

MRS. BOYLE. It's the job of the hospital to save life, not to lose it.

KEN. The hospital's done all it can, but it wasn't enough. It wasn't the hospital's fault; the original injury was too big.

MRS. BOYLE. We have to make the best of the situation.

KEN. No. *We* don't have to do anything. I have to do what is to be done and that is to cash in the chips.

MRS. BOYLE. It's not unusual, you know, for people injured as you have been, to suffer with this depression for a considerable time before they begin to see that a life is possible.

KEN. How long?

MRS. BOYLE. It varies.

KEN. Don't hedge.

MRS. BOYLE. It could be a year or so.

KEN. And it could last for the rest of my life.

MRS. BOYLE. That would be most unlikely.

KEN. I'm sorry, but I cannot settle for that.

MRS. BOYLE. Try not to dwell on it. I'll see what I can do to get you started on some occupational therapy. Perhaps we could make a start on the reading machines.

KEN. Do you have many books for those machines?

MRS. BOYLE. Quite a few.

KEN. Can I make a request for the first one?

MRS. BOYLE. If you like.

KEN. "How to be a Sculptor with no Hands."

MRS. BOYLE. I'll be back tomorrow with the machine.

KEN. It's marvelous you know.

MRS. BOYLE. What is?

KEN. All you people have the same technique. When I say something really awkward you just pretend I haven't said anything at all. You're all the bloody same... Well, there's another outburst. That should be your cue to comment on the light-shade or the color of the walls.

MRS. BOYLE. I'm sorry if I have upset you.

KEN. Of course you have upset me. You and the doctors with your appalling so-called professionalism, which is nothing more than a series of verbal tricks to prevent you relating to your patients as human beings.

MRS. BOYLE. You must understand; we have to remain relatively detached in order to help ...

KEN. That's all right with me. Detach yourself. Tear yourself off on the dotted line that divides the woman from the social worker and post yourself off to another patient.

MRS. BOYLE. You're very upset ...

KEN. Christ Almighty, you're doing it again. Listen to yourself, woman. I say something offensive about you and you turn your professional cheek. If you were human, if you were treating me as a human, you'd tell me to bugger off. Can't you see that this is why I've decided that life isn't worth living? I am not human and I'm even more convinced of that by your visit than I was before, so how does that grab you? The very exercise of your so-called professionalism makes me want to die.

MRS. BOYLE. I'm ... Please ...

KEN. Go ... For God's sake, get out ... Go on ... Get out ... Get out.

(She goes into SISTER's room. SISTER hears KEN's shouts.)

SISTER. What's the matter, Mrs. Boyle?

MRS. BOYLE. It's Mr. Harrison ... He seems very upset.

KEN *(shouting).* ... I am upset. *(SISTER closes the door.)*

SISTER. I should leave him for now, Mrs. Boyle. We'll send for you again when he's better. *(SISTER hurries in to KEN. He is very distressed, rocking his head from side to side, desperately short of breath.)*

KEN. Sis ... ter ... *(SISTER reaches for the oxygen mask.)*

SISTER. Now, now, Mr. Harrison, calm down. *(She applies the mask and turns on the oxygen. KEN gradually becomes calmer.)* Now why do you go getting yourself so upset? ... There's no point ...

KEN *(muffled).* But ...

SISTER. Stop talking, Mr. Harrison. Just relax.

(KEN becomes calm. SISTER sees NURSE SADLER going past. MRS. BOYLE is still hovering.)

SISTER. Nurse.

NURSE. Sister?

SISTER. Take over here, will you?

NURSE. Yes, Sister. *(NURSE SADLER holds the mask. SISTER goes to the door.)*

MRS. BOYLE. Is he all right?

SISTER. Yes, perfectly.

MRS. BOYLE. I'm sorry ...

SISTER. Don't worry. It was not you ... We'll let you know when he's better.

MRS. BOYLE. Right ... Thank you. *(She goes. SISTER stands at the open door.)*

SISTER. Just give him another ten seconds, Nurse.

NURSE. Yes, Sister. *(SISTER takes a pace back behind the door and listens. After ten seconds, NURSE SADLER removes the mask.)*

KEN. Oh, she's a shrewd cookie, is our Sister. *(SISTER smiles at this. NURSE SADLER glances backward. KEN catches on to the reason.)* It's all right, Sister. I'm still alive, bugger it. I don't want to give her too much satisfaction.

NURSE. She's gone. *(She closes the door.)*

KEN. Come on then, over here. I shan't bite you, Kay. Come and cool my fevered brow or something.

NURSE. What upset you?

KEN. Being patronized, I suppose.

NURSE. What did you mean about Sister?

KEN. She knew if she came in I'd shout at her, but if you were here I wouldn't shout.

NURSE. Why?

KEN. A good question. Because I suppose you're young and gentle and innocent and Sister knows that I am not the sort who would shout at you...

NURSE. You mean, you would rather patronize me.

KEN. Hey! Steady on there, Kay. If you show you're well able to take care of yourself I shall have to call you Nurse Sadler and shout at you, too, and Sister and I will have lost a valuable asset.

NURSE. What were you?...

(The door opens and SISTER and DR. SCOTT come in.)

KEN. What is this? Piccadilly Circus?

SISTER. All right, Nurse. Dr. Scott was just coming as it happened. Are you feeling better now, Mr. Harrison? *(NURSE SADLER leaves.)*

KEN. Lovely, thank you, Sister.

SISTER. I made your phone call to Mr. Hill. He said he'd try to get in tomorrow.

KEN. Thank you ... *(SISTER leaves.)*

DR. SCOTT. And what was all the fuss about?

KEN. I'm sorry about that. The last thing I want is to bring down Emerson again with his pharmaceutical truncheon.

DR. SCOTT. I'm ... sorry about that.

KEN. I don't suppose it was your fault.

DR. SCOTT. Can I give you some advice?

KEN. Please do; I may even take it.

DR. SCOTT. Take the tablets; the dose is very small—the minimum—and it won't really blunt your consciousness, not like the injection.

KEN. ... You're on.

DR. SCOTT. Good ... I was glad to hear about your decision to try and get your compensation settled.

KEN. How did you? ... Oh, I suppose Sister checked with you.

DR. SCOTT. She did mention it ...

KEN. You have lovely breasts.

DR. SCOTT. I beg your pardon?

KEN. I said you have lovely breasts.

DR. SCOTT. What an odd thing to say.

KEN. Why? You're not only a doctor are you? You can't tell me that you regard them only as mammary glands.

DR. SCOTT. No.

KEN. You're quite safe.

DR. SCOTT. Of course.

KEN. I'm not about to jump out of bed and rape you or anything.

DR. SCOTT. I know.

KEN. Did it embarrass you?

DR. SCOTT. Surprised me.

KEN. And embarrassed you.

DR. SCOTT. I suppose so.

KEN. But why exactly? You are an attractive woman. I admit that it's unusual for a man to compliment a woman on her breasts when only one of them is in bed, only one of the people, that is, not one of the breasts, but that wasn't the reason, was it?

DR. SCOTT. I don't think it helps you to talk like this.

KEN. Because I can't do anything about it, you mean.

DR. SCOTT. I didn't mean that exactly.

KEN. I watch you walking in the room, bending over me, tucking in your sweater. It's surprising how relaxed a woman can become when she is not in the presence of a man.

DR. SCOTT. I am sorry if I provoked you ... I can assure you ...

KEN. You haven't "provoked" me as you put it, but you are a woman and even though I've only a piece of knotted string between my legs, I still have a man's mind. One change that I have noticed is that I now engage in sexual banter with young nurses, searching for the double entendre in the most innocent remark. Like a sexually desperate middle-aged man. Then they leave the room and I go cold with embarrassment. It's fascinating, isn't it? Laughable. I still have tremendous sexual desire. Do you find that disgusting?

DR. SCOTT. No.

KEN. Pathetic?

DR. SCOTT. Sad.

KEN. I am serious, you know ... about deciding to die.

DR. SCOTT. You will get over that feeling.

KEN. How do you know?

DR. SCOTT. From experience.

KEN. That doesn't alter the validity of my decision now.

DR. SCOTT. But if we acted on your decision now, there wouldn't be an opportunity for you to accept it.

KEN. I grant you, I may become lethargic and quiescent. Happy when a nurse comes to put in a new catheter, or give me an enema, or to turn me over. These could become the high spots of my day. I might even learn to do wonderful things, like turn the pages of a book with some miracle of modern science, or to type letters by flicking my eyelids. And you would look at me and say: "Wasn't it worth waiting?" And I would say: "Yes" and be proud of my achievements. Really proud. I grant you all that, but it doesn't alter the validity of my present position.

DR. SCOTT. But if you became happy?

KEN. But I don't want to become happy by becoming the computer section of a complex machine. And morally, you must accept my decision.

DR. SCOTT. Not according to my morals.

KEN. And why are yours better than mine? They're better because you're more powerful. I am in your power. To hell with a morality that is based on the proposition that might is right.

DR. SCOTT. I must go now. I was halfway through Mr. Patel. *(She walks to the door.)*

KEN. I thought you were just passing. Oh, Doctor... one more thing...

DR. SCOTT. Yes?

KEN. You still have lovely breasts.

(She smiles and goes out into the SISTER's office. She is very upset. SISTER passes and looks at her.)

SISTER. Are you all right? Would you like a cup of tea?

DR. SCOTT. Yes, Sister, I would.

SISTER. ... Nurse? Would you bring a cup of tea, please.

(NURSE SADLER looks from the kitchen.)

NURSE. Yes, Sister. *(They walk into the SISTER's room and sit down.)*

DR. SCOTT. I've never met anyone like Ken Harrison before.

SISTER. No.

DR. SCOTT. He's so ... bright ... intelligent ... He says he wants to die.

SISTER. Many patients say that

DR. SCOTT. I know that, Sister, but he means it. It's just a calm rational decision.

SISTER. I thought this morning, when he was talking about the compensation, he was beginning to plan for the future.

DR. SCOTT. Not really, you know. That was just to keep us happy. He probably thinks that if he pretends to be planning for the future, we'll stop tranquilizing him or something like that. *(A knock at the door.)*

SISTER. Come in.

(NURSE SADLER enters.)

NURSE. Here's the tea, Sister.

SISTER. Thank you, Nurse. For Doctor. *(NURSE SADLER gives the cup to DR. SCOTT and goes out.)*

DR. SCOTT. It's marvelous, you know. We bring him back to life using everything we've got. We give him back his consciousness, then he says, "But how do I use it?" So what do we do? We put him back to sleep.

(CROSSFADE on KEN's room. JOHN goes in to empty the rubbish. He taps KEN lightly as if to repeat the steel band game, but KEN is asleep.)

JOHN. Ping-pong ... You poor bastard. *(He leaves.)*

END OF ACT ONE

ACT TWO

SISTER. A visitor for you, Mr. Harrison.

HILL. Good afternoon, Mr. Harrison.

KEN. Good afternoon.

HILL. You're looking very much better. *(SISTER has placed a chair by the bed.)*

KEN. It's the nursing, you know.

SISTER. I'm glad you realize it, Mr. Harrison.

KEN. Oh, I do, Sister, I do.

SISTER. I'll leave you gentlemen now.

HILL. Thank you, Sister. *(She goes out.)* You really do look better.

KEN. Yes. I'm as well now as I shall ever be...

HILL *(unzipping his briefcase)*. I've brought all the papers... Things are moving along very satisfactorily now and...

KEN. I don't want to talk about the accident.

HILL. I understand it must be very distressing...

KEN. No, no. It's not that. I didn't get you here about the compensation.

HILL. Oh... Sister said on the phone...

KEN. Yes, I know. Could you come away from the door? Look, do you work for yourself? I mean, you don't work for an insurance company or something, do you?...

HILL. No. I'm in practice as a solicitor, but I...

42

KEN. Then there's no reason why you couldn't represent me generally ... apart from this compensation thing.

HILL. Certainly, if there's anything I can do ...

KEN. There is.

HILL. Yes?

KEN. ... Get me out of here.

HILL. ... I don't understand, Mr. Harrison

KEN. It's quite simple. I can't exist outside the hospital, so they've got me to keep me here if they want to keep me alive and they seem intent on doing that. I've decided that I don't want to stay in the hospital any longer.

HILL. But surely they wouldn't keep you here longer than necessary?

KEN. I'm almost completely paralyzed and I always will be. I shall never be discharged by the hospital. I have coolly and calmly thought it out and I have decided that I would rather not go on. I therefore want to be discharged to die.

HILL. And you want me to represent you?

KEN. Yes. Tough.

HILL. ... And what is the hospital's attitude?

KEN. They don't know about it yet. Even tougher.

HILL. This is an enormous step ...

KEN. Mr. Hill, with all respect, I know that our hospitals are wonderful. I know that many people have succeeded in making good lives with appalling handicaps. I'm happy for them and respect and admire them. But each man must make his own decision. And mine is to die quietly and with as much dignity as I can muster and I need your help.

HILL. Do you realize what you're asking me to do?

KEN. I realize. I'm not asking that you make any decision about my life and death, merely that you represent me and my views to the hospital.

HILL. ... Yes, well, the first thing is to see the doctor. What is his name?

KEN. Dr. Emerson

HILL. I'll try and see him now and come back to you.

KEN. Then you'll represent me? ...

HILL. Mr. Harrison, I'll let you know my decision after I've seen Dr. Emerson.

KEN. All right, but you'll come back to tell me yourself, even if he convinces you he's right?

HILL. Yes, I'll come back.

(CROSSFADE on the sluice room. NURSE SADLER and JOHN are talking.)

JOHN. So why not? ...

NURSE. It's just that I'm so busy ...

JOHN. All work and no play ... makes for a boring day.

NURSE. Anyway, I hardly know you.

JOHN. Right ... That's why I want to take you out ... to find out what goes on behind those blues eyes ...

NURSE. At present, there's just lists of bones and organs, all getting themselves jumbled up.

JOHN. Because you're working too hard ...

NURSE. Ask me next week ...

JOHN. Okay. It's a deal ...

NURSE. Right!

JOHN. And I'll ask you this afternoon as well.

(CROSSFADE on DR. EMERSON's office.)

DR. EMERSON. Mr. Hill? Sister just rang through.

HILL. Dr. Emerson? *(They shake hands.)*

DR. EMERSON. You've been seeing Mr. Harrison?

HILL. Yes.

DR. EMERSON. Tragic case...I hope you'll be able to get enough money for him to ease his mind.

HILL. Dr. Emerson. It's not about that I wanted to see you. I thought I was coming about that, but Mr. Harrison wishes to retain me to represent him on quite another matter.

DR. EMERSON. Oh?

HILL. Yes, he wants to be discharged.

DR. EMERSON. That's impossible.

HILL. Why?

DR. EMERSON. To put it bluntly, he would die if we did that.

HILL. He knows that. It's what he wants.

DR. EMERSON. And you are asking me to kill my patient?

HILL. I am representing Mr. Harrison's wishes to you and asking for your reaction.

DR. EMERSON. Well, you've had it. It's impossible. Now if that's really all you came about...

HILL. Dr. Emerson, you can, of course, dismiss me like that if you choose to, but I would hardly think it serves anyone's interests, least of all Mr. Harrison's.

DR. EMERSON. I am trying to save Mr. Harrison's life. There is no need to remind me of my duty to my patient, Mr. Hill.

HILL. Or mine to my client, Dr. Emerson.

DR. EMERSON. ... Are you telling me that you have accepted the job of coming to me to urge a course of action that will lose your client his life?

HILL. I hadn't accepted it ... no ... I told Mr. Harrison I would talk to you first. Now I have and I begin to see why he thought it necessary to be represented.

DR. EMERSON. All right ... Let's start again. Now tell me what you want to know.

HILL. Mr. Harrison wishes to be discharged from the hospital. Will you please make the necessary arrangements?

DR. EMERSON. No.

HILL. May I ask why not?

DR. EMERSON. Because Mr. Harrison is incapable of living outside the hospital and it is my duty as a doctor to preserve life.

HILL. I take it that Mr. Harrison is a voluntary patient here.

DR. EMERSON. Of course.

HILL. Then I fail to see the legal basis for your refusal.

DR. EMERSON. Can't you understand that Mr. Harrison is suffering from depression? He is incapable of making a rational decision about his life and death.

HILL. Are you maintaining that Mr. Harrison is mentally unbalanced?

DR. EMERSON. Yes.

HILL. Would you have any objection to my bringing in a psychiatrist for a second opinion?

DR. EMERSON. Of course not, but why not ask the consultant psychiatrist here? I'm sure he will be able to convince you.

HILL. Has he examined Mr. Harrison?

DR. EMERSON. No, but that can be quickly arranged.

HILL. That's very kind of you, Dr. Emerson, but I'm sure you'll understand if I ask for my own—whose opinion you are not sure of *before* he examines the patient.

DR. EMERSON. Good afternoon, Mr. Hill.

HILL. Good afternoon. *(MR. HILL takes up his briefcase and leaves.)*

DR. EMERSON *(picking up the phone)*. Could you find out where Dr. Travers is, please? I want to see him urgently, and put me through to the hospital secretary, please. Well, put me through when he's free.

(CROSSFADE on KEN's room. The door opens and MR. HILL comes in.)

KEN. Well, how was it on Olympus?

HILL. Cloudy.

KEN. No joy then?

HILL. Dr. Emerson does not wish to discharge you.

KEN. Surprise, surprise. So what do we do now?

HILL. Mr. Harrison, I will be perfectly plain. Dr. Emerson claims that you are not in a sufficiently healthy mental state to make a rational decision, especially one of this seriousness and finality. Now my position is, I am not competent to decide whether or not he is right.

KEN. So how will you decide?

HILL. I should like to have you examined by an independent psychiatrist and I will accept his view of the case and advise you accordingly.

KEN. Fair enough. Will Dr. Emerson agree?

HILL. He has already. I ought to warn you that Dr. Emerson is likely to take steps to have you admitted here as a person needing treatment under the Mental Health Act of

1959. This means that he can keep you here and give you what treatment he thinks fit.

KEN. Can he do that?

HILL. He probably can.

KEN. Haven't I any say in this?

HILL. Oh, yes. He will need another signature and that doctor will have to be convinced that you ought compulsorily to be detained. Even if he agrees, we can appeal.

KEN. Let's get on with it, then.

HILL. One thing at a time. First, you remember, our own psychiatrist.

KEN. Wheel him in...

HILL. I'll be in touch soon, then.

KEN. Oh, before you go. Yesterday I refused to take a tranquilizer and Dr. Emerson came and gave me an injection. It made me pretty dopey. If I was like that when the psychiatrist came, he'd lock me up for life!

HILL. I'll mention it to him. Goodbye for now, then.

KEN. Goodbye.

(CROSSFADE on DR. EMERSON's office. DR. EMERSON is on the phone. DR. TRAVERS knocks on his door and looks in.)

DR. EMERSON. Can you find me Dr. Scott, please? *(He puts the phone down.)*

DR. TRAVERS. You wanted to see me?

DR. EMERSON. Ah yes. If you can spare a moment.

DR. TRAVERS. What's the problem?

DR. EMERSON. Nasty one really, I have a road accident case paralyzed from the neck down. He's naturally very depressed and wants to discharge himself. But with a neurogenic bladder and all the rest of it, he couldn't last a week out of here. I need time to get him used to the idea.

DR. TRAVERS. How long ago was the accident?

DR. EMERSON. Six months.

DR. TRAVERS. A long time.

DR. EMERSON. Yes, well there were other injuries, but we've just about got him physically stabilized. The trouble is that he's got himself a solicitor and if I am to keep him here, I'll have to admit him compulsorily under the Mental Health Act. I wondered if you'd see him.

DR. TRAVERS. I'll see him, of course, but my signature won't help you.

DR. EMERSON. Why not? You're the psychiatrist, aren't you?

DR. TRAVERS. Yes, but under the Act, you need two signatures and only one can come from a practitioner of the hospital where the patient is to be kept.

DR. EMERSON. Bloody hell!

DR. TRAVERS. Not to worry. I take it you regard this as an emergency.

DR. EMERSON. Of course, I do.

DR. TRAVERS. Well, sign the application and then you've got three days to get another signature.

DR. EMERSON. There'll be no problem about that surely?

DR. TRAVERS. Depends on whether he's clinically depressed or not.

DR. EMERSON. You haven't understood. He's suicidal. He's determined to kill himself.

DR. TRAVERS. I could name you several psychiatrists who wouldn't take that as evidence of insanity.

DR. EMERSON. Well, I could name several psychiatrists who *are* evidence of insanity. I've had a lot of experience in this kind of case. I'm sure, absolutely sure, I can win him around, given time ... a few months ...

DR. TRAVERS. I understand, Michael.

DR. EMERSON. ... So you'll look at him, will you? ... And get another chap in? ...

DR. TRAVERS. Yes, I'll do that.

DR. EMERSON *(twinkling)*. And ... do me a favor, will you? Try and find an old codger like me, who believes in something better than suicide.

DR. TRAVERS *(grinning)*. There's a chap at Ellertree ... a very staunch Catholic, I believe. Would that suit you?

DR. EMERSON. Be Jasus—sounds just the man!

DR. TRAVERS. I'll see his notes and drop in on him ...

DR. EMERSON. Thank you very much, Paul ... I'm very grateful ... and Harrison will be, too.

(DR. SCOTT comes in the room.)

DR. SCOTT. Oh, sorry.

DR. TRAVERS. It's all right ... I'm just off ... I'll see him then, Michael, this afternoon. *(DR. TRAVERS leaves. DR. SCOTT looks at DR. EMERSON questioningly.)*

DR. SCOTT. You wanted me?

DR. EMERSON. Ah, yes. Harrison's decided to discharge himself.

DR. SCOTT. Oh, no, but I'm not surprised.

DR. EMERSON. So, Travers is seeing him now.

DR. SCOTT. Dr. Travers won't make him change his mind.

DR. EMERSON. I am committing him under Section 26.

DR. SCOTT. Oh, will Dr. Travers sign it?

DR. EMERSON. Evidently if I do, he can't, but he knows a chap over in Ellertree who probably will.

DR. SCOTT. I see

DR. EMERSON. I have no choice, do you see, Joan? He's got himself a solicitor. It's the only way I can keep him here.

DR. SCOTT. Are you sure you should?

DR. EMERSON. Of course. No question.

DR. SCOTT. It's his life.

DR. EMERSON. But my responsibility.

DR. SCOTT. Only if he's incapable of making his own decision.

DR. EMERSON. But he isn't capable. I refuse to believe that a man with a mind as quick as his, a man with enormous mental resources, would calmly choose suicide.

DR. SCOTT. But he has done just that.

DR. EMERSON. And, therefore, I say he is unbalanced.

DR. SCOTT. But surely a wish to die is not *necessarily* a symptom of insanity? A man might want to die for perfectly sane reasons.

DR. EMERSON. No, Joan, a doctor cannot accept the choice for death; he's committed to life. When a patient is brought into my unit, he's in a bad way. I don't stand about thinking whether or not it's worth saving his life. I haven't the time for doubts. I get in there, do whatever I can to save life. I'm a doctor, not a judge.

DR. SCOTT. I hope you will forgive me, sir, for saying this, but I think that is just how you are behaving—as a judge.

DR. EMERSON. You must, of course, say what you think—but I am the responsible person here.

DR. SCOTT. I know that, sir. *(She makes to go.)*

DR. EMERSON. I'm sure it's not necessary for me to say this but I'd rather there was no question of misunderstanding later...Mr. Harrison is now physically stable. There is no reason why he should die; if he should die suddenly, I would think it necessary to order a post-mortem and to act on whatever was found.

DR. SCOTT. ...Mr. Harrison is your patient, sir.

DR. EMERSON *(smiling)*. Of course, of course. You make that sound a fate worse than death.

DR. SCOTT. Perhaps for him it is. *(She goes out.)*

(CROSSFADE on KEN's room. DR. TRAVERS comes in.)

DR. TRAVERS. Mr. Harrison?

KEN. That's right.

DR. TRAVERS. Dr. Travers.

KEN. Are you a psychiatrist?

DR. TRAVERS. Yes.

KEN. For or against me...Or does that sound like paranoia?

DR. TRAVERS. You'd hardly expect me to make an instant diagnosis.

KEN. Did Dr. Emerson send you?

DR. TRAVERS. I work here, in the hospital.

KEN. Ah.

DR. TRAVERS. Would you describe yourself as suffering from paranoia?

KEN. No.

DR. TRAVERS. What would you say paranoia was?

KEN. Difficult. It depends on the person. A man whose feelings of security are tied to his own sense of what is right and can brook no denial. If he were, say, a sculptor, then we would describe his mental condition as paranoia. If, on the other hand, he was a doctor, we would describe it as professionalism.

DR. TRAVERS (laughing). You don't like doctors!

KEN. Do you like patients?

DR. TRAVERS. Some.

KEN. I like some doctors.

DR. TRAVERS. What's wrong with doctors, then?

KEN. Speaking generally, I suppose that as a profession, you've not learnt that the level of awareness of the population has risen dramatically; that black magic is no longer much use and that people *can* and *want* to understand what's wrong with them and many of them can make decisions about their own lives.

DR. TRAVERS. What they need is information.

KEN. Of course, but as a rule, doctors dole out information like a kosher butcher gives out pork sausages.

DR. TRAVERS. That's fair. But you'd agree that patients need medical knowledge to make good decision?

KEN. I would. Look at me, for example. I'm a sculptor, an airy-fairy artist, with no real hard knowledge and no capability to understand anything about my body. You're a doctor but I think I would hold my own with a competition in anatomy with you.

DR. TRAVERS. It's a long time since I did any anatomy.

KEN. Of course. Whereas I was teaching it every day up to six months ago. It wouldn't be fair.

DR. TRAVERS. Your knowledge of anatomy may be excellent, but what's your neurology like, or your dermatology, endocrinology, urology, and so on?

KEN. Lousy, and insofar as these bear on my case, I should be grateful for information so that I can make a proper decision. But it is my decision. If you came to my studio to buy something, and look at all my work, and you say: "I want that bronze" and I say to you: "Look, you don't know anything about sculpture. The proportion of that is all wrong, the texture is boring and it should have been made in wood anyway. You are having the marble!" you'd think I was nuts. If you were sensible you'd ask for my professional opinion but if you were a mature adult, you'd reserve the right to choose for yourself.

DR. TRAVERS. But we're not talking about a piece of sculpture to decorate a room, but about your life.

KEN. That's right, Doctor. *My* life.

DR. TRAVERS. But your obvious intelligence weakens your case. I'm not saying that you would find life easy but you do have resources that an unintelligent person doesn't have.

KEN. That sounds like Catch 22. If you're clever and sane enough to put up an invincible case for suicide, it demonstrates you ought not to die. *(DR. TRAVERS moves the stool near the bed.)* That's a disturbing tidiness compulsion you've got there.

DR. TRAVERS. I was an only child; enough of me. Have you any relationships outside the hospital?... You're not married, I see.

KEN. No, thank God.

DR. TRAVERS. A girl friend?

KEN. A fiancée, actually. I asked her not to visit me anymore. About a fortnight ago.

DR. TRAVERS. She must have been upset.

KEN. Better that than a lifetime's sacrifice.

DR. TRAVERS. She wanted to ... stay with you, then?

KEN. Oh yes ... Had it all worked out ... But she's a young,
healthy woman. She wants babies ... real ones. Not one
that never *will* learn to walk.

DR. TRAVERS. But if that's what she really wants.

KEN. Oh, come on, Doctor. If that's what she really wants,
there's plenty of other cripples who want help. I told her
to go to release her, I hope, from the guilt she would feel
if she did what she really wanted to.

DR. TRAVERS. That's very generous.

KEN. Balls. Really, Doctor, I did it for *me*. It would destroy *my* self-respect if I allowed myself to become the
object with which people can safely exploit their maso-
chist tendencies.

DR. TRAVERS. That's putting it very strongly.

KEN. Yes. Too strongly. But you are beginning to sound
like the chaplain. He was in here the other day. He
seemed to think I should be quite happy to be God's
chosen vessel into which people could pour their com-
passion ... That it was all right being a cripple because it
made other folk feel good when they helped me.

DR. TRAVERS. What about your parents?

KEN. Working-class folk—they live in Scotland. I thought
it would break my mother—I always thought of my father as a very tough egg. But it was the other way round.
My father can only think with his hands. He used to
stand around here completely at a loss. My mother
would sit there—just understanding. She knows what

suffering's about. They were here a week ago—I got rid of my father for a while and told my mother what I was going to do. She looked at me for a minute. There were tears in her eyes. She said, "Aye, lad, it's thy life...don't worry about your dad—I'll get him over it."...She stood up and I said: "What about you?" "What about me?" she said, "Do you think life's so precious to me, I'm frightened of dying?"...I'd like to think I was my mother's son.

DR. TRAVERS. ... Yes, well, we shall have to see.

KEN. What about? You mean you haven't made up your mind?

DR. TRAVERS. ... I shall have to do some tests...

KEN. What tests, for Christ's sake? I can tell you now, my time over a hundred metres is lousy.

DR. TRAVERS. You seem very angry.

KEN. Of course I'm angry...No, no...I'm...Yes, I am angry. *(Breathing.)* But I am trying to hold it in because you'll just write me off as in a manic phase of a manic depressive cycle.

DR. TRAVERS. You are very free with psychiatric jargon.

KEN. Oh, well then, you'll be able to say I'm an obsessive hypochondriac. *(Breathing.)*

DR. TRAVERS. I certainly wouldn't do that, Mr. Harrison.

KEN. Can't you see what a trap I am in? Can anyone prove that they are sane? Could you?

DR. TRAVERS. ... I'll come and see you again.

KEN. No, don't come and see me again, because every time you come, I'll get more and more angry, and more and more upset and depressed. And eventually you will destroy my mind.

DR. TRAVERS. I'm sorry if I upset you, Mr. Harrison.

(DR. TRAVERS replaces the stool and exits. He crosses to the SISTER's office. Enter DR. SCOTT and MR. HILL.)

DR. SCOTT. I hate the idea. It's against all my training and instincts...

HILL. Mine, too. But in this case, we're not dealing with euthanasia, are we?

DR. SCOTT. Something very close.

HILL. Something very far away. Suicide.

DR. SCOTT. Thank you for a lovely meal.

HILL. Not at all, I am glad you accepted. Tell me, what would you think, or rather feel, if there was a miracle and Ken Harrison was granted the use of his arms for just one minute and he used them to grab a bottle of sleeping tablets and swallowed the lot?

DR. SCOTT. ...It's irrational but...I'd be very...relieved.

HILL. It wouldn't go against your instincts?...You wouldn't feel it was a wasted life and fight with stomach pumps and all that?

DR. SCOTT. No...not if it was my decision.

HILL. You might even be sure there *was* a bottle of tablets handy and you not there.

DR. SCOTT. You make it harder and harder...but, yes, I might do that...

HILL. Yes. Perhaps we ought to make suicide respectable again. Whenever anyone kills himself there's a whole legal rigmarole to go through—investigations, inquests and so on—and it all seems designed to find someone or something to *blame*. Can you ever recall a coroner saying something like: "We've heard all the evidence of how John Smith was facing literally insuperable odds and he made a courageous decision. I record a verdict of a noble death"?

DR. SCOTT. No ... it's been a ... very pleasant evening.

HILL. Thank you. For me, too.

DR. SCOTT. I don't know if I've helped you, though.

HILL. You have. I've made up my mind.

DR. SCOTT. You'll help him?

HILL. Yes ... I hope you're not sorry.

DR. SCOTT. I'm pleased ...

HILL. I'm sure it is morally wrong for anyone to try to hand the responsibility for their death to anyone else. And it's wrong to accept that responsibility, but Ken isn't trying to do that.

DR. SCOTT. I'm glad you've made up your mind ... Good night. (*They stop.*)

HILL. I hope I see you again.

DR. SCOTT. I'm in the phone—Good night.

HILL. Good night.

(*They exit. NURSE SADLER goes into KEN's room with a meal.*)

KEN. You still on duty?

NURSE. We're very short-staffed ... (*She's prepared to feed KEN with a spoon.*) It looks good tonight ... Minced beef.

KEN. Excellent ... and what wine shall we order then? How about a '48 claret. Yes, I think so ... Send for the wine waiter.

NURSE. You are a fool, Mr. Harrison.

KEN. Is there any reason why I shouldn't have wine?

NURSE. I don't know. I'll ask Sister if you like ...

KEN. After all, the hospital seems determined to depress my consciousness. But they'd probably think it's immoral if I enjoy it. *(NURSE SADLER gives him a spoonful of mince.)* It's a bit salty.

NURSE. Do you want some water?

KEN. That would be good. Very nice... Not too full of body. Chateau Ogston Reservoir, I think, with just a cheeky little hint of Jeyes fluid from the sterilizer.

NURSE. We use Milton.

KEN. Oh dear... you'd better add to my notes. The final catastrophe. Mr. Harrison's palate is failing; rush up the emergency resuscitation unit. *(In a phony American accent.)* Nurse, give me orange... No response... Quick the lemon... God! Not a flicker... We're on the tightrope... Nurse pass the ultimate... Quick, there's no time to lose... Pass the hospital mince. That would bring people back from the dead. Don't tell Emerson that or he'll try it. I don't want anymore of that.

(NURSE SADLER exits. DR. SCOTT comes in.)

KEN. Sister.

DR. SCOTT. No, it's me. Still awake?

KEN. Yes.

DR. SCOTT. It's late.

KEN. What time is it?

DR. SCOTT. Half past eleven.

KEN. The night Sister said I could have the light for half an hour. I couldn't sleep. I wanted to think.

DR. SCOTT. Yes.

KEN. You look lovely.

DR. SCOTT. Thank you.

KEN. Have you been out?

DR. SCOTT. For a meal.

KEN. Nice. Good company?

DR. SCOTT. You're fishing

KEN. That's right.

DR. SCOTT. Yes, it was good company.

KEN. A colleague?

DR. SCOTT. No. Actually it was Philip Hill, your solicitor.

KEN. Well, well, well...The randy old devil. He didn't take long to get cracking, did he?

DR. SCOTT. It was just a dinner.

KEN. I know I engaged him to act for me. I didn't realize he would see his duties so comprehensively.

DR. SCOTT. It was just a dinner!

KEN. Well, I hope my surrogate self behaved myself.

DR. SCOTT. You were a perfect gentleman.

KEN. Mm...then perhaps I'd better engage another surrogate.

DR. SCOTT. Do you mind really?

KEN. ...No. Unless you convinced him that Emerson was right.

DR. SCOTT. ...I didn't try.

KEN. Thank you.

DR. SCOTT. I think you are enjoying all this.

KEN. I suppose I am in a way. For the first time in six months I feel like a human being again.

DR. SCOTT. Yes. (A pause.) Isn't that the whole point, Ken, that...

KEN. You called me Ken.

DR. SCOTT. Do you mind?

KEN. Oh! No, I liked it. I'll just chalk it up as another credit for today.

DR. SCOTT. I was saying, isn't that just the point; isn't that what this fight has shown you? That you are a human being again. You're not fighting for death. I don't think you want to win.

KEN. That was what I had to think about.

DR. SCOTT. And have you ... changed your mind?

KEN. ... No. I know I'm enjoying the fight and I had to be sure that I wanted to win, really get what I'm fighting for, and not just doing it to convince myself I'm still alive.

DR. SCOTT. And are you sure?

KEN. Yes, quite sure; for me life is over. I want it recognized because I can't do the things that I want to do. That means I can't say the things I want to say. Is that a better end? You understand, don't you?

(NURSE SADLER comes in with a feeding cup.)

NURSE. I didn't know you were here, Doctor.

DR. SCOTT. Yes, I'm just going.

KEN. See what I mean, Doctor. Here is my substitute mum, with her porcelain pap. This isn't for me.

DR. SCOTT. No ...

KEN. So tomorrow, on with the fight!

DR. SCOTT. Good night ... and good luck.

(FADE.)

KERSHAW. So our psychiatrist is prepared to state that Harrison is sane.

HILL. Yes, he was sure. I'll have his written report tomorrow. He said he could understand the hospital fighting to save their patient from himself, but no matter how much he sympathized with them and how much he wished he could get Harrison to change his mind, nevertheless, he was sane and knew exactly what he was doing and why he was doing it.

KERSHAW. And you say that the hospital is holding him under Section 26?

HILL. Yes, they rang me this morning. They got another chap in from Ellertree to sign it as well as Emerson.

KERSHAW. Hm... Tricky. There's no precedent for this, you know. Fascinating.

HILL. Yes.

KERSHAW. And you're sure in your mind he knows what he's doing?

HILL. Yes.

KERSHAW. ... Well ... Let's see him, shall we?

HILL. Here's the Sister's office.

KERSHAW. Is she your standard gorgon?

HILL. Only on the outside. but under that iron surface beats a heart of stainless steel.

(They go into SISTER's office.)

HILL. Good morning, Sister.

SISTER. Morning, Mr. Hill.

HILL. This is a colleague, Mr. Kershaw.

SISTER. Good morning.

KERSHAW. Good morning.

HILL. Is it all right to see Mr. Harrison? ...

SISTER. Have you asked Dr. Emerson?

HILL. Oh, yes ... before we came ...

SISTER. I see ...

HILL. You can check with him...

SISTER. ...I don't think that's necessary...However, I'm afraid I shall have to ask you if I can stay with Mr. Harrison while you interview him.

HILL. Why?

SISTER. We are very worried about Mr. Harrison's mental condition, as you know. Twice recently he has...got excited...and his breathing function has not been able to cope with the extra demands. Dr. Emerson has ordered that at any time Mr. Harrison is subjected to stress, someone must be there as a precaution.

HILL. ...I see. *(He glances at MR. KERSHAW, who shrugs.)* Very well.

SISTER. This way, gentlemen.

(They go into KEN's room.)

HILL. Good morning, Mr. Harrison.

KEN. Morning.

HILL. I've brought along Mr. Kershaw. He is the barrister who is advising us.

KERSHAW. Good morning, Mr. Harrison.

HILL. Your doctor has insisted that Sister remains with us—to see you don't get too excited.

KEN. Oh! Sister, you know very well that your very presence always excites me tremendously. It must be the white apron and black stockings. A perfect mixture of mother and mistress. *(SISTER grins a little sheepishly and takes a seat at the head of the bed. KEN strains his head to look at her. SISTER turns back the covers.)* Sister, what are you doing! Oh. Just for a minute there, Sister...*(SISTER takes his pulse.)*

HILL. ... Well ...

SISTER. Just a moment, Mr. Hill ... *(She finishes taking the pulse.)* Very well.

KEN. So, Mr. Kershaw, what is your advice? *(MR. KERSHAW pauses. MR. HILL makes to speak, but MR. KERSHAW stops with a barely perceptible shake of the head. A longer pause.)*

KERSHAW. ... If you succeed in your aim you will be dead within a week.

KEN. I know.

KERSHAW. ... I am informed that without a catheter the toxic substance will build up in your bloodstream and you will be slowly poisoned by your own blood.

KEN *(smiles)*. ... You should have brought along a tape recorder. That speech would be much more dramatic with sound effects!

KERSHAW *(relaxing and smiling)*. I had to be sure you know what you are doing.

KEN. I know.

KERSHAW. And you have no doubt whatsoever; no slightest reservations? ...

KEN. None at all.

KERSHAW. Let's look at the possibilities. You are now being held under the Mental Health Act, Section 26, which means they can keep you here and give you any treatment they believe you need. Under the law we can appeal to a tribunal.

KEN. How long will that take?

KERSHAW. ... Up to a year.

KEN. A year! A year! Oh God, can't it be quicker than that?

KERSHAW. It might be quicker, but it could be a year.

KEN. Jesus Christ! I really would be crazy in a year.

KERSHAW. That's the procedure.

KEN. I couldn't stay like this for another year, I couldn't.

HILL. We could always try habeas corpus.

KERSHAW. That would depend if we could find someone.

KEN. Habeas corpus? What's that? I thought it was something to do with criminals.

KERSHAW. Well, it usually is, Mr. Harrison. Briefly, it's against the law to deprive anyone of their liberty without proper cause. If anyone is so deprived, they or a friend can apply for a writ of habeas corpus, which is the Latin for "You may have the body."

KEN. Particularly apt in my case.

KERSHAW. ...the people who are doing the detaining have to produce the...person, before the judge and if they can't give a good enough reason for keeping him, the judge will order that he be released.

KEN. It sounds as if it will take as long as that tribunal you were talking about.

KERSHAW. No. Habeas corpus is one of the very few legal processes that move very fast. We can approach any judge at any time even when the courts aren't sitting and he will see that it's heard straight away—in a day or so usually.

HILL. If you could find a judge to hear it.

KEN. Why shouldn't a judge hear it.

KERSHAW. Habeas corpus itself is fairly rare. This would be rarer.

KEN. Will I have to go to court?

KERSHAW. I doubt it. The hearing can be in court or in private, in the judge's chambers, as we say. The best thing to do in this case is for Mr. Hill and me to find a judge, issue the writ, then we'll get together with the hospital's barrister and we'll approach the judge together and suggest we hold the subsequent hearing here.

KEN. In this room?

KERSHAW. I expect the judge will agree. If he ordered you to be produced in court and anything happened to you, it would be a classical case of prejudging the issue.

KEN. I wouldn't mind.

KERSHAW. But the judge would feel rather foolish. I should think it would be in a few days.

KEN. Thank you. It'll be an unusual case for you—making a plea for the defendant's death.

KERSHAW. I'll be honest with you. It's a case I could bear to lose.

KEN. If you do—it's a life sentence for me.

KERSHAW. Well, we shall see. Good morning, Mr. Harrison. *(They go out with the SISTER. They pause at the SISTER's office.)*

HILL. Thank you very much, Sister...I'm very sorry about all this. I do realize it must be upsetting for you.

SISTER. Not at all, Mr. Hill. As I have a stainless steel heart, it's easy to keep it sterilized of emotion. Good morning. *(She goes into her room. HILL and KERSHAW go out.)*

(CROSSFADE on KEN's room. JOHN and NURSE SADLER are setting chairs for the hearing. JOHN begins to sing "Dry Bones.")

NURSE. John!

JOHN. What's the matter? *(NURSE SADLER is confused.)*

NURSE. Nothing, of course...silly...*(KEN picks up the vibes between the two.)*

KEN. Hello, hello...What have we here? Don't tell me that Cupid has donned his antiseptic gown and is flying the corridors of the hospital, shooting his hypodermic syringes into maidens' hearts...

NURSE. No!

KEN. John?

JOHN. Honestly, your honor, I'm not guilty. I was just walking down the corridor when I was struck dumb by the beauty of this nurse.

NURSE. Don't be an idiot, John...We need an extra chair...Can you go and find one, please?

JOHN. Your wishes, oh, queen, are my command. *(He bows and goes out.)*

NURSE. He is a fool.

KEN. He isn't. He's been bloody good to me. Have you been out with him?...It's none of my business, of course.

NURSE. We went to a club of his last night...He plays in a band, you know.

KEN. Yes, I know.

NURSE. They're really good. They should go a long way...Still, I shouldn't be going on like this.

KEN. Why not?...Because I'm paralyzed? Because I can't go dancing?

NURSE. Well...

KEN. The other day I was low and said to John, who was shaving me, I was useless, what could I do? I served no purpose and all the rest of the whining miseries. John set about finding things I could do. He said, first, because I could move my head from side to side *(KEN does so.)* I could be a tennis umpire; then as my head was going, I could knock a pendulum from side to side and keep a clock going. Then he said I could be a child-minder and because kids were always doing what they shouldn't, I could be perpetually shaking my head. He went on and on getting more and more fantastic—like radar scanners. I laughed so much that the Sister had to rush in and give me oxygen.

NURSE. He *is* funny.

KEN. He's more than that. He's free!

NURSE. Free?

KEN. Free of guilt. Most everybody here feels guilt about me—including you. That's why you didn't want to tell me what a fantastic time you had dancing. So everybody makes me feel worse because I make them feel guilty. But not John. He's sorry for me but he knows bloody well it isn't his fault. He's a tonic.

(JOHN comes back carrying SISTER's armchair.)

NURSE. John! Did Sister say you could have that chair?

JOHN. She wasn't there...

NURSE. She'll kill you; no one ever sits in her chair.

JOHN. Why? Is it contaminated or something? I just thought that if the poor old judge had to sit here listening to that miserable bugger moaning on about wanting to die, the least we could do was to make him comfortable.

KEN *(laughing to NURSE SADLER)*. See? *(JOHN sits in the chair and assumes a grave face.)*

JOHN. Now, this is a very serious case. The two charges are proved...Firstly, this hospital has been found guilty of using drugs to make people happy. That's terrible.

Next, and most surprising of all, this hospital, in spite of all their efforts to the contrary, are keeping people alive! We can't have that. *(Footsteps outside.)*

NURSE. Sister's coming!

(JOHN jumps up and stands between the chair and the door. SISTER comes in and as she approaches the bed with her back to the chair, JOHN slips out of the room.)

KEN. Well, now, we have some very important visitors today, Sister.

SISTER. Indeed, we have.

KEN. Will you be here?

SISTER. No.

KEN. I feel a bit like a traitor.

SISTER. ...We all do what we've got to.

KEN. That's right, but not all of us do it as well as you, Sister...

SISTER. ...Thank you.

(SISTER moves to go. DR. SCOTT comes in.)

DR. SCOTT. Good morning, Sister.

SISTER *(brightly)*. Good morning. *(She goes quickly without noticing the chair. DR. SCOTT watches her go.)*

KEN. I've upset her, I'm afraid.

DR. SCOTT. You shouldn't do that. She is a marvelous Sister. You ought to see some of the others.

KEN. That's what I told her.

DR. SCOTT. Oh, I see. Well, I should think that's just about the one way past her defenses. How are you this morning?

KEN. Fine.

DR. SCOTT. And you're going ahead with it?

KEN. Of course.

DR. SCOTT. Of course.

KEN. I haven't had any tablets, yesterday or today.

DR. SCOTT. No.

KEN. Thank you.

DR. SCOTT. Thank the judge. He ordered it.

KEN. Ah!

(DR. EMERSON comes in.)

DR. EMERSON. Good morning, Mr. Harrison.

KEN. Morning, Doctor.

DR. EMERSON. There's still time.

KEN. No, I want to go on with it ... unless you'll discharge me.

DR. EMERSON. I'm afraid I can't do that. The judge and lawyers are conferring. I thought I'd just pop along and see if you were all right. We've made arrangements for the witnesses to wait in the Sister's office. I am one, so I should be grateful if you would remain here, with Mr. Harrison.

DR. SCOTT. Of course.

DR. EMERSON. Well, I don't want to meet the judge before I have to. I wish you the best of luck, Mr. Harrison, so that we'll be able to carry on treating you.

KEN *(smiling).* Thank you for your good wishes *(DR. EMERSON nods and goes out.)*

DR. SCOTT. If I didn't know *you* I'd say *he* was the most obstinate man I've ever met.

(As DR. EMERSON makes for his office, MR. HILL comes down the corridor.)

HILL. Good morning.

DR. EMERSON. Morning. *(MR. HILL stops and calls after DR. EMERSON.)*

HILL. Oh, Dr. Emerson...

DR. EMERSON. Yes?

HILL. I don't know...I just want to say how sorry I am that you have been forced into such a...distasteful situation.

DR. EMERSON. It's not over yet, Mr. Hill. I have every confidence that the law is not such an ass that it will force me to watch a patient of mine die unnecessarily.

HILL. We are just as confident that the law is not such an ass that it will allow anyone arbitrary power.

DR. EMERSON. My power isn't arbitrary; I've earned it with knowledge and skill and it's also subject to the laws of nature.

HILL. And to the laws of the state.

DR. EMERSON. If the state is so foolish as to believe it is competent to judge a purely professional issue.

HILL. It's always doing that. Half the civil cases in the calendar arise because someone is challenging a professional's opinion.

DR. EMERSON. I don't know about other professions but I do know this one: medicine, is being seriously threatened because of the intervention of law. Patients are becoming so litigious that doctors will soon be afraid to offer any opinion or take any action at all.

HILL. Then they will be sued for negligence.

DR. EMERSON. We can't win.

HILL. Everybody wins. You wouldn't like to find yourself powerless in the hands of, say, a lawyer or a ... bureaucrat. I wouldn't like to find myself powerless in the hands of a doctor.

DR. EMERSON. You make me sound as if I were some sort of Dracula ...

HILL. No! ... I for one certainly don't doubt your good faith but in spite of that I wouldn't like to place *anyone* above the law.

DR. EMERSON. I don't want to be above the law; I just want to be under laws that take full account of professional opinion.

HILL. I'm sure it will do that, Dr. Emerson. The questions is, whose professional opinion?

DR. EMERSON. We shall see.

(MR. ANDREW EDEN, the hospital's barrister, and MR. HILL and MR. KERSHAW come into KEN's room.)

HILL. Morning, Mr. Harrison. This is Mr. Eden who will be representing the hospital.

KEN. Hello.

(They settle themselves into the chairs. The SISTER enters with the JUDGE.)

SISTER. Mr. Justice Millhouse.

JUDGE. Mr. Kenneth Harrison?

KEN. Yes, my Lord.

JUDGE. This is an informal hearing which I want to keep as brief as possible. You are, I take it, Dr. Scott?

DR. SCOTT. Yes, my Lord.

JUDGE. I should be grateful, Doctor, if you would interrupt the proceedings at any time you think it necessary.

DR. SCOTT. Yes, my Lord.

JUDGE. I have decided in consultation with Mr. Kershaw and Mr. Hill that we shall proceed thus: I will hear a statement from Dr. Michael Emerson as to why he believes Mr. Harrison is legally detained, and then a statement from Dr. Richard Barr, who will support the application. We have decided not to subject Mr. Harrison to examination and cross-examination.

KEN. But I...

JUDGE (*sharply*). Just a moment, Mr. Harrison. If, as appears likely, there remains genuine doubt as to the main issue, I shall question Mr. Harrison myself. Dr. Scott, I wonder if you would ask Dr. Emerson to some in.

DR. SCOTT. Yes, my Lord. (*She goes out.*) Would you come in now, sir.

(*SISTER brings DR. EMERSON into KEN's room.*)

JUDGE. Dr. Emerson, I would like you to take the oath. (*The JUDGE hands DR. EMERSON a card with the oath written on it.*)

DR. EMERSON. I swear the evidence that I give shall be the truth, the whole truth and nothing but the truth.

JUDGE. Stand over there, please. (*The JUDGE nods to MR. EDEN.*)

EDEN. You are Dr. Michael Emerson?

DR. EMERSON. I am.

EDEN. And what is your position here?

DR. EMERSON. I am a consultant physician and in charge of the intensive care unit.

EDEN. Dr. Emerson, would you please give a brief account of your treatment of this patient.

DR. EMERSON *(referring to notes)*. Mr. Harrison was admitted here on the afternoon of October 9th, as an emergency following a road accident. He was suffering from a fractured left tibia and right tibia and fibia, a fractured pelvis, four fractured ribs, one of which had punctured the lung, and dislocated fourth vertebra, which had ruptured the spinal cord. He was extensively bruised and had minor lacerations. He was deeply unconscious and remained so for thirty hours. As a result of treatment, all the broken bones and ruptured tissue have healed with the exception of a severed spinal cord and this, together with a mental trauma, is now all that remains of the initial injury.

EDEN. Precisely, Doctor. Let us deal with those last two points. The spinal cord. Will there be any further improvements in that?

DR. EMERSON. In the present state of medical knowledge, I would think not.

EDEN. And the mental trauma you spoke of?

DR. EMERSON. It's impossible to injure the body to the extent that Mr. Harrison did and not affect the mind. It is common in these cases that depression and the tendency to make wrong decisions goes on for months, even years.

EDEN. And in your view Mr. Harrison is suffering from such a depression?

DR. EMERSON. Yes.

EDEN. Thank you, Doctor.

JUDGE. Mr. Kershaw?

KERSHAW. Doctor. Is there any objective way you could demonstrate this trauma? Are there, for example, the results of any test, or any measurements you can take to show it to us.

DR. EMERSON. No.

KERSHAW. Then how do you distinguish between a medical syndrome and a sane, even justified, depression?

DR. EMERSON. By using my thirty years' experience as a physician, dealing with both types.

KERSHAW. No more questions, my Lord.

JUDGE. Mr. Eden, do you wish to re-examine?

EDEN. No, my Lord.

JUDGE. Thank you, Doctor. Would you ask Dr. Barr if he would step in please? (DR. EMERSON goes out.)

DR. EMERSON. It's you now, Barr.

(SISTER brings DR. BARR into KEN's room.)

SISTER. Dr. Barr.

JUDGE. Dr. Barr, will you take the oath please. (He does so.) Mr. Kershaw.

KERSHAW. You are Dr. Richard Barr?

DR. BARR. I am.

KERSHAW. And what position do you hold?

DR. BARR. I am a consultant psychiatrist at Norwood Park Hospital.

KERSHAW. That is primarily a mental hospital, is it not?

DR. BARR. It is.

KERSHAW. Then you must see a large number of patients suffering from depressive illness.

DR. BARR. I do, yes.

KERSHAW. You have examined Mr. Harrison?

DR. BARR. I have, yes.

KERSHAW. Would you say that he was suffering from such an illness?

DR. BARR. No, I would not.

KERSHAW. Are you quite sure, Doctor?

DR. BARR. Yes, I am.

KERSHAW. The court has heard evidence that Mr. Harrison is depressed. Would you dispute that?

DR. BARR. No, but depression is not necessarily an illness. I would say that Mr. Harrison's depression is reactive rather than endogenous. That is to say, he is reacting in a perfectly rational way to a very bad situation.

KERSHAW. Thank you, Dr. Barr.

JUDGE. Dr. Eden?

EDEN. Dr. Barr. Are there any objective results that you could produce to prove Mr. Harrison is capable?

DR. BARR. There are clinical symptoms of endogenous depression, of course, disturbed sleep patterns, loss of appetite, lassitude, but even if they were present, they would be masked by the physical condition.

EDEN. So how can you be sure this *is* in fact just a reactive depression?

DR. BARR. Just by experience, that's all, and by discovering when I talk to him that he has a remarkably incisive mind and is perfectly capable of understanding his position and of deciding what to do about it.

EDEN. One last thing, Doctor; do you think Mr. Harrison has made the right decision?

KERSHAW (*quickly*). Is that really relevant, my Lord? After all ...

JUDGE. Not really ...

DR. BARR. I should like to answer it, though.

JUDGE. Very well.

DR. BARR. No, I thought he made the wrong decision. *(To KEN.)* Sorry.

EDEN. No more questions, my Lord.

JUDGE. Do you wish to re-examine, Mr. Kershaw?

KERSHAW. No, thank you, my Lord.

JUDGE. That will be all, Dr. Barr. *(DR. BARR goes out. The JUDGE stands. To KEN.)* Do you feel like answering some questions?

KEN. Of course.

JUDGE. Thank you.

KEN. You are too kind.

JUDGE. Not at all.

KEN. I mean it. I'd prefer it if you were a hanging judge.

JUDGE. There aren't any anymore.

KEN. Society is now much more sensitive and humane?

JUDGE. You could put it that way.

KEN. I'll settle for that.

JUDGE. I would like you to take the oath. Dr. Scott, his right hand please. *(KEN takes the oath.)* The consultant physician here has given evidence that you are not capable of making a rational decision.

KEN. He's wrong.

JUDGE. Why then do you think he came to that opinion?

KEN. He's a good doctor and won't let a patient die if he can help it.

JUDGE. He found that you were suffering from acute depression.

KEN. Is that surprising? I am almost totally paralyzed. I'd be insane if I *weren't* depressed.

JUDGE. But there is a difference between being unhappy and being depressed in the medical sense.

KEN. I would have thought that my psychiatrist answered that point.

JUDGE. But, surely, wishing to die must be strong evidence that the depression has moved beyond a mere unhappiness into a medical realm?

KEN. I don't wish to die.

JUDGE. Then what is this case all about?

KEN. Nor do I wish to live at any price. Of course I want to live but as far as I am concerned, I'm dead already. I merely require the doctors to recognize the fact. I cannot accept this condition constitutes life in any real sense at all.

JUDGE. Certainly, you're alive legally.

KEN. I think I could challenge even that.

JUDGE. How?

KEN. Any reasonable definition of life must include the idea of its being self-supporting. I seem to remember something in the papers—when all the heart transplant controversy was on—about it being all right to take someone's heart if they require constant attention from respirators and so on to keep them alive.

JUDGE. There also has to be absolutely no brain activity at all. Yours is certainly working.

KEN. It is and sanely.

JUDGE. That is the question to be decided.

KEN. My Lord, I am not asking anyone to kill me. I am only asking to be discharged from this hospital.

JUDGE. It comes to the same thing.

KEN. Then that proves my point; not just the fact that I will spend the rest of my life in the hospital, but that while I am here, everything is geared just to keeping my brain active, with no real possibility of it ever being able to direct anything. As far as I can see, that is an act of deliberate cruelty.

JUDGE. Surely, it would be more cruel if society let people die, when it could, with some effort, keep them alive.

KEN. No, not *more* cruel, *just* as cruel.

JUDGE. Then why should the hospital let you die—if it is just as cruel?

KEN. The cruelty doesn't reside in saving someone or allowing them to die. It resides in the fact that the choice is removed from the man concerned.

JUDGE. But a man who is very desperately depressed is not capable of making a reasonable choice.

KEN. As you said, my Lord, that is the question to be decided.

JUDGE. All right. You tell me why it is a reasonable choice that you decided to die.

KEN. It is a question of dignity. Look at me here. I can do nothing, not even the basic primitive functions. I cannot even urinate, I have a permanent catheter attached to me. Every few days my bowels are washed out. Every few hours two nurses have to turn me over or I would rot away from bedsores. Only my brain functions unimpaired but even that is futile because I can't act on any conclusions it comes to. This hearing proves that. Will you please listen.

JUDGE. I am listening.

KEN. I choose to acknowledge the fact that I am in fact dead and I find the hospital's persistent effort to maintain this shadow of life an indignity and it's inhumane.

JUDGE. But wouldn't you agree that many people with appalling physical handicaps have overcome them and lived essentially creative, dignified lives?

KEN. Yes, I would but the dignity starts with their choice. If I choose to live, it would be appalling if society killed me. If I choose to die, it is equally appalling if society keeps me alive.

JUDGE. I cannot accept that it is undignified for society to devote resources to keeping someone alive. Surely it enhances that society.

KEN. It is not undignified if the man wants to stay alive, but I must restate that the dignity starts with his choice. Without it, it is degrading because technology has taken over from human will. My Lord, if I cannot be a man, I do not wish to be a medical achievement. I'm fine...I am fine.

JUDGE. It's all right. I have no more questions. *(The JUDGE stands up and walks to the window. He thinks a moment.)* This is a most unusual case. Before I make a judgment I want to state that I believe all the parties have acted in good faith. I propose to consider this for a moment. The law on this is fairly clear. A deliberate decision to embark on a course of action that will lead inevitably to death is not *ipso facto* evidence of insanity. If it were, society would have to reward many men with a dishonorable burial rather than a posthumous medal for gallantry. On the other hand, we do have to bear in mind that Mr. Harrison has suffered massive physical injuries and it is possible that his mind is affected. Any judge in his career will have met men who are without doubt insane in the meaning of the Act and yet appear in the witness box to be rational. We must, in this case, be most careful not to allow Mr. Harrison's obvious wit and intelligence to blind us to the fact that he could be suffering from a depressive illness...and so we have to face the disturbing fact of the divided evidence ... and bear in mind that, however much we may sympathize with Mr. Harrison in his cogently argued case to be allowed to die, the law instructs us to ignore it if it is the product of a disturbed or clinically depressed mind ... However, I am satisfied that Mr. Harrison is a brave and cool man who is in complete control of his mental faculties and I shall therefore make an order for him to be set free. *(A pause. The JUDGE walks over to KEN.)* Well, you got your hanging judge!

KEN. I think not, my Lord. Thank you. *(The JUDGE nods and smiles.)*

JUDGE. Goodbye.

(He turns and goes. He meets DR. EMERSON in the SISTER's room. While he talks to him, everyone else, except DR. SCOTT, comes out.)

JUDGE. Ah, Dr. Emerson.

DR. EMERSON. My Lord?

JUDGE. I'm afraid you'll have to release your patient.

DR. EMERSON. I see.

JUDGE. I'm sorry. I understand how you must feel.

DR. EMERSON. Thank you.

JUDGE. If ever I have to have a road accident, I hope it's in this town and I finish up here.

DR. EMERSON. Thank you again.

JUDGE. Goodbye.

(He walks down the corridor. DR. EMERSON stands a moment then slowly goes back to the room. KEN is looking out of the window. DR. SCOTT is sitting by the bed.)

DR. EMERSON. Where will you go?

KEN. I'll get a room somewhere.

DR. EMERSON. There's no need.

KEN. Don't let's ...

DR. EMERSON. We'll stop treatment, remove the drops. Stop feeding you if you like. You'll be unconscious in three days, dead in six at most.

KEN. There'll be no last-minute resuscitation?

DR. EMERSON. Only with your express permission.

KEN. That's very kind; why are you doing it?

DR. EMERSON. Simple! You might change your mind.

KEN *(smiles and shakes his head)*. Thanks. I won't change my mind, but I'd like to stay. *(DR. EMERSON nods and goes. DR. SCOTT stands and moves to the door.)* You were right, you know. He really is a most obstinate man! *(DR. SCOTT turns and moves to KEN as if to kiss him.)* Oh, don't, but thank you. *(DR. SCOTT smiles weakly and goes out. The lights are held for a long moment, and then snap out.)*

END OF PLAY

PRODUCTION NOTES

THE SET

The set may be a complex multiple construction, but probably more effectively it will consist of various areas controlled by light. Three of these are essential: Ken's room, the Sister's office, and the Consultant's office.

Ken's room is at center stage, his bed a bit right of center. The Sister's office is at left. Between these two areas is a corridor running up and downstage, with an exit ULC. Dr. Emerson's office is UR, presumably reached via an arm of the corridor. At DL is an exit to the kitchen.

The furniture in these areas need consist only of essential pieces: bed, desks and chairs. The locker in Ken's room is optional; if it is not used, the Sister may simply carry a card with her and produce it at the proper time. Practical doors to the various rooms are not necessary; knocking, opening, etc., may all be pantomimed. If actual doors are used, care should be taken not to obstruct sight line.

PROPERTIES

GENERAL: Ken's room: Hospital bed with pillows, sheets, etc.; chart and notes at foot of bed; locker (optional) with card in it. In Act Two, several extra chairs will be needed. Sister's office: Desk and chair, telephone and writing materials on desk, another chair. Small tray containing pill and feeding cup with water; syringes, vials of medicines, kidney dishes and other medical equipment. Dr. Emerson's office: Desk and chair, telephone, writing materials and papers on desk.

PERSONAL:

    SISTER - Wheeled cart containing alcohol, talcum powder, etc.

    JOHN - Shaving equipment on tray (electric shaver).

    DR. SCOTT - Stethoscope.

    NURSE - Feeding cup containing milk drink.

    DR. EMERSON - Notes.

    MR. HILL - Briefcase.

    NIGHT NURSE - Feeding cup.

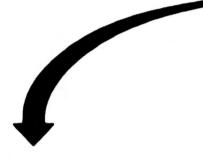

WHOSE LIFE IS IT ANYWAY?

"A blazing light in this season."
Richard Eder
New York Times

"A very wise and funny play."
Clive Barnes
New York Post

"An overwhelming tribute to life."
Gene Shalit
NBC-TV

DIRECTOR'S NOTES

DIRECTOR'S NOTES

DIRECTOR'S NOTES